EARLY LEARNING EXPERIENCES IN FOLLOWING DIRECTIONS

by Imogene Forte and Joy MacKenzie

Incentive Publications, Inc.
Nashville, Tennessee

Illustrated by Gayle Seaberg Harvey
Edited by Jan Keeling

ISBN 0-86530-326-6

Table Of Contents

About This Book . . .

Early Learning Experiences in Following Directions has been planned to help young children learn through experimentation, through creative involvement in directed activities, and finally, through the joy of discovery.

Young children are curious about and extremely sensitive to their environment. They instinctively push and pull, take apart and attempt to put together again, smell, taste, feel, and listen to things around them. "Why?" "What?" "When?" "Where?" and "How?" are words they use naturally and often. It is this interaction with their environment that parents and teachers can either nurture and encourage or inhibit and retard. Children who have had many happy, satisfying opportunities to use their hands, feet, eyes, ears, and whole bodies are much more apt to adjust happily and successfully to more structured learning experiences.

The purposes of the activities in *Early Learning Experiences in Following Directions* are to help children understand and appreciate their environment, to develop self-awareness, to express themselves creatively, and to provide enjoyment and appreciation of literature.

The book includes a mix of simple hands-on activities, free-choice activities, and more structured teacher-directed activities. While instructions are directed to the child, an adult will, of course, need to read and interact with the child in the interpretation and completion of the activities. Ideally, the projects will be presented in a stress-free setting that will afford time for the child to question, explore, wonder, ponder, and create—and to develop an abiding, imaginatively inquisitive approach to creative self-expression. The fanciful illustrations will provide added incentive for lively interaction. Each activity is intended to contribute to the development of skills and concepts which will enhance the child's self-concept and serve as a guide to personal achievement.

Paper Talk

You can make a piece of paper talk!
Follow the directions below to make a duck who can quack.
Then you can use the same idea to make all kinds of talking creatures.

1. Cut on the dotted line to remove the bottom section of this page.

2. Fold on the solid line to make what looks like a greeting card.

3. Cut from the star on the folded edge to the star near the middle of the card.

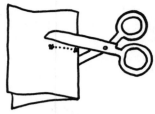

4. Fold back the flaps to form two triangles.

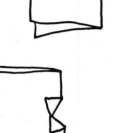

5. Open the card like this.

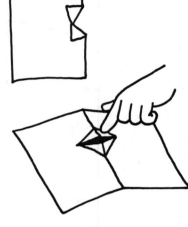

6. Put your finger on one triangle and push it carefully through to the other side of the card. Then do the same thing to the other triangle.

7. Close your card. It will look like this on the outside.

8. When you open the card, it will look like this on the inside.

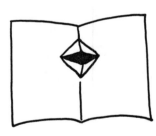

9. When you open and close the card, it will look like a talking mouth.

10. Now draw a funny duck head around the talking mouth, and you will have a quacking duck. Color your duck.

How to Make a Peanut Butter Sandwich

Do you know how to make a peanut butter sandwich?
Try to explain it to someone who has never made one before.
Don't leave out any detail that that person would need to know.

As you tell how to make the sandwich, ask a real person to record
or write your directions on the sandwich below.

Now follow your own directions to make a real sandwich.
Were your directions clear and complete?
Cut your sandwich in half and share it with a friend.
See if you can sing with your mouth full of sandwich!

My Name Is _____

Can't See Simon

You probably have played a game of "Simon Says" before—but
have you ever done it when you couldn't see Simon?
Invite one or more friends or classmates to play this game with you.
You will need a blindfold.

1. Choose one friend to be "IT" and to wear the blindfold.
2. Place "IT" at one side of the room and carefully turn his or
    her body around several times.
3. Then take turns giving "IT" instructions to move from his or
    her place to a particular place across the room. Guide your
    friend ("IT") safely by calling out good directions.
4. After arriving safely to the chosen place, "IT" should remove
    the blindfold and choose the next person to be "IT."

Take two
small steps
forward ....

Balloon Bunches

Choose four crayons, each one a different color.
Use the four crayons to color all the balloons on this page.
Try NOT to color any two balloons that are next to each
other the same color.
Put your crayons away and find a pencil.
Use your pencil to make into a bunch each group
of balloons that match in color.

Example: Draw a string from each blue balloon to the same point
and make a bow. Then all the blue balloons will be "tied together."

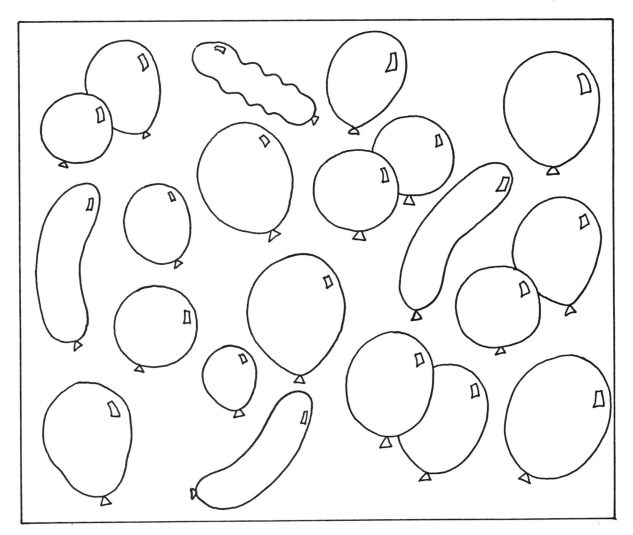

How many different balloon bunches did you make?

My Name Is _____

13

Rainbow Roundup

Color and cut out this beautiful rainbow.
Paste your rainbow on the following page.
Use your crayons to color a blue sky all around it.
Color the sun above the rainbow golden.

Long ago, storytellers said that if you could find the
end of a rainbow you would see a pot of gold.

Imagine how a pot of gold would look and draw your
imaginary pot of gold at the rainbow's end.

Make up a story about the person who finds this
pot of gold and tell what they will do with it!

My Name Is _____

"Big Wind" Regatta

Follow these directions to prepare your racing boat for the "Big Wind" Regatta.

You will need:

- scissors
- crayons
- tape
- a pinch of clay or play dough
- a coffee stirrer or toothpick
- a large cake pan or lasagna pan with about one inch of water in it
- drinking straws

1. Use capital letters to write the initials of your name on the sail. (Write carefully on the line.)
2. Color the sail and the boat if you wish.
3. Cut out the sail and the boat.
4. Fold tabs on the dotted lines and tape together to form the body of the boat.
5. Press a pinch of clay or play dough onto the X in the center of the boat.
6. Tape the long side of the sail to the coffee stirrer or toothpick.
7. Hoist your sail in the pinch of clay and set your boat on the water at one end of the "lake" (the pan with an inch of water).
8. Ask a friend to set his or her boat at the opposite end of the lake.
9. At a signal, blow through your drinking straws to make your boats travel to the opposite ends of the lake.
10. The one who reaches the other end of the lake first wins the regatta.

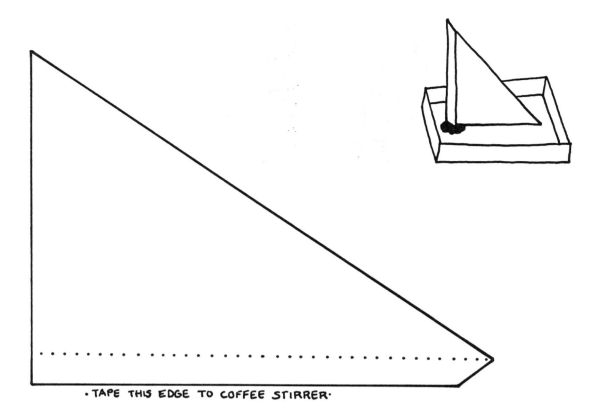

· TAPE THIS EDGE TO COFFEE STIRRER ·

✕

17

Mix-up, Match-up

Cut carefully on the dotted lines to make a set of eighteen
"Mix-up, Match-up" character cards.

1. Spread the cards on a table or floor.
2. Choose one body and see if you can find a head card and a foot card to go with it.
3. Continue to match body parts until you have six complete characters.

NOTE: You can make a game by shuffling the cards and dividing them into two groups. Keep one group and give a friend or classmate the other. Then see who can use the cards to make the most complete characters the fastest.

OR

You may use the cards to create funny, make-believe, mixed-up characters just for a giggle.

Sammy Squirrel's Message

Follow these directions to solve Sammy Squirrel's puzzle.

1. Cross out the O in the third box in the first row.
2. Dot the I in the fourth box in the first row.
3. Write E in the second box in the second row.
4. Cross the T in the first box in the fourth row.
5. Name the letters in the second and third boxes in the fourth row. Cross them out.
6. Read the message.
7. Draw some nuts for Sammy.

My Name Is _____

Shape Shuffle

Cut on the dotted lines to separate the shape cards.

1. Study each card to see which of the following shapes is represented by the card. Name the shape.
2. Arrange the shape cards in piles or groups of like shapes.
3. Use the empty boxes to create a shape picture of your own to go with each group.

To create a card game, shuffle the cards and divide them among several friends or classmates.

1. Take turns being the leader. When the leader lays out a card, each of the other players must search his or her pile to find one card that represents the same shape.
2. The players should place their similar cards next to the leader's card.
3. Then the person to the right of the leader becomes the leader and plays a card.
4. Continue until all cards are played.

Body Games

Invite some friends to join you in a musical listening game.
Practice singing the songs on this page or other
similar songs you may know.
As you sing, listen to the words and act out the
proper motions for each line.

Head and Shoulders, Knees and Toes
(Use both hands to touch each body part as it is mentioned.)

Head and shoulders, knees and toes, knees and toes,
Head and shoulders, knees and toes, knees and toes,
Eyes and ears and lips and cheeks and nose,
Head and shoulders, knees and toes, knees and toes.

If You're Happy and You Know It
(Listen to hear how you should move each body part.)

If you're happy and you know it, clap your hands.
If you're happy and you know it, clap your hands.
If you're happy and you know it, why not let your body show it!
If you're happy and you know it, clap your hands.

Verse 2: Stamp your feet.
Verse 3: Shake your head.
Verse 4: Shout "Hooray!"

Wet Sandwich, Dry Sandwich

Have you ever made a sandwich in a jar?
You can make a wet sandwich or a dry sandwich.
Follow the directions on these pages to make one of each!

A Wet Sandwich

1. Find a clean jar with a very secure lid.

2. Carefully pour the liquids listed below into the jar. Put them into the jar in the following order:

   1st: glycerin
   2nd: light yellow corn or peanut oil
   3rd: wine vinegar and oil salad dressing
   4th: water, tinged with a little green or blue food coloring.

3. Put the top on the jar and let it stand still for a while. Soon you will be able to clearly see the layers of your liquid sandwich.

A Dry Sandwich

1. Find a tall jar with a secure lid.

2. One at a time, carefully pour into the jar a layer of several different dry ingredients. You may choose from the list below or think of some other ingredients on your own!

   - sand
   - rice
   - beans
   - cereal
   - salt
   - macaroni or small pasta pieces

   Choose items that are colorful and make an attractive display of shapes and textures.

3. Put the lid on the jar.

4. Use your jar as a paperweight or a shelf decoration.

Jar sandwiches also make wonderful gifts!

Your Name in Silver!

You don't need a pencil, a pen, a marker, or a crayon to write your name. You can write it with almost any kind of object.
If you had a space that was large enough (and a driver's license), you could write your name using school buses!
You would just line up the buses in the shape of your name.

1. Find a group of objects that are all *smaller* than a school bus (probably not larger than a table knife).
2. Spread a big sheet of paper on the floor or table.
3. Arrange the group of objects on the paper so that the objects form the shapes of the letters of your name.
4. Glue the objects to the paper. If the objects are too heavy for gluing, trace around them with a crayon or marker and color the shapes fancy or pretty or wild!

Some Ideas for Objects
  plastic silverware
  drinking straws
  peanuts in the shell
  toothpicks
  leaves and sticks
  pretzels, crackers, or doughnuts
  flowers
  footprints or pawprints
  sponges
  candies
  paper clips
  coins

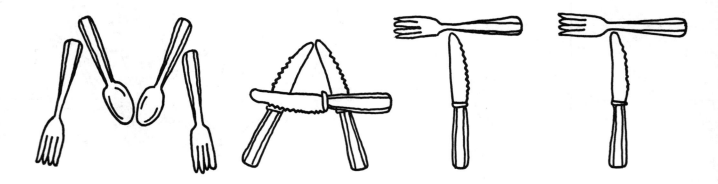

Making Magic

Wouldn't it be fun to be able to make wishes come true?
In fairy tales, a magic wand can make things appear or disappear, or
the wand can spread fairy dust that causes magical things to happen.
Of course a wand can't really do that, but it is such fun to pretend!

Follow the directions to make your very own personal magic wand.

You will need:
- a long stick or a dowel
- crepe paper or ribbon
- scraps of fabric and colored paper
- a gift bow
- decorations like sequins, stickers, or confetti
- tape

1. Wrap the stick in strips of fabric or crepe paper.
2. Glue some sequins, stickers, or confetti pieces to the stick.
3. Make streamers of ribbon and attach them to the tip of the stick.
4. Attach a gift bow at the other end of the stick.
5. Wave your beautiful wand and see what magic may happen!

A Fine Feathered Friend

If you carefully follow the directions below, you will soon see a fancy feathered friend appear, as if by magic!

You will need:
- about 4 tablespoons of birdseed
- a thick paper towel
- a rubber band
- a small glass of water
- colored construction paper
- tape

1. Spread the paper towel on a table.
2. Place the birdseed in the center of the paper towel.
3. Carefully bring the corners of the towel together and fasten with a rubber band so that the seed is tightly sealed inside.
4. Place the ends of the paper towel down inside the glass of water. Rest the ball of birdseed on the top edge of the glass.
5. After a few days, the seeds will begin to sprout and what looks like a bird with a feathered head will appear!
6. Glue a tiny triangle of yellow or orange paper on the edge of the glass to make the bird's beak.
7. Cut some plumes of colored paper to attach to the back side of the glass to make the bird a fancy tail.

Double-dip Poetry

A Poem for Two Voices or Two Groups of Voices

This activity may be performed by two
people, two groups, or a leader and a group.
Practice reading or reciting the poem
until the words and parts are familiar.
Then recite the poem as a choral reading exercise.
Vary your voices so some parts are loud and
some are almost whispers.
Can you see the fireflies in your imagination?

VOICE 1	VOICE 2
LIGHT!	LIGHT!
Tiny flashes of light.	Blinking . . . blinking.
Streaks in the night.	Little yellow streaks.
Flitting . . .	Flitting . . .
Flashing!	Flashing!
Gleaming . . .	Gleaming . . .
Glowing . . .	Glowing . . .
Artists in flight,	Little blinking artists,
Painting with bright brushes	On the dark night.
Swish!	Swish!
Flickering here.	Flashing there.

Fireflies

Just Like the Movies!

You can make some cartoons!

Follow these directions:

1. Cut apart the following pages on the dotted lines.

2. Stack the cartoon pictures in order, beginning with #1 on the top and ending with #24 on the bottom.

3. As you stack, put a drop of glue on the X on each page. Be sure each page is placed exactly on top of the other.

4. Secure the stack of pictures by taping around the end of the stack where the X's appear.

5. Now hold the stack in your hands and flip the frames of the cartoon from front to back and watch the cartoon. You can make it go backwards by flipping from back to front!

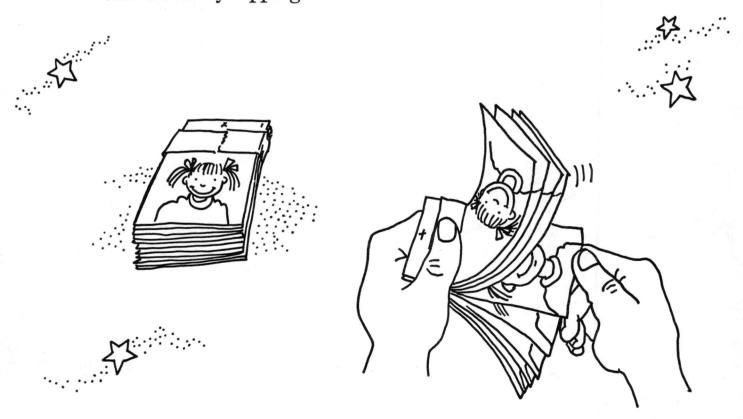

Fold-away Problems

Use the strips on the next page to write and solve
your own subtraction problems.

1. Cut on the solid lines to separate the strips.
2. Use Strip #1 as a test strip to practice a subtraction problem.
   Count the items on the strip. How many are there?
3. Now decide how many you would like to subtract.
4. Fold the end of the strip back under to the left so that the strip
   hides your chosen number of items.
5. How many items are left? Count them.

Can you write a number story?

Choose a new strip and write a number story to go
with the subtraction problem.

Give each of your friends or classmates a strip and see how many
different number stories you all can create.

Use your strips to share your number stories with one another.

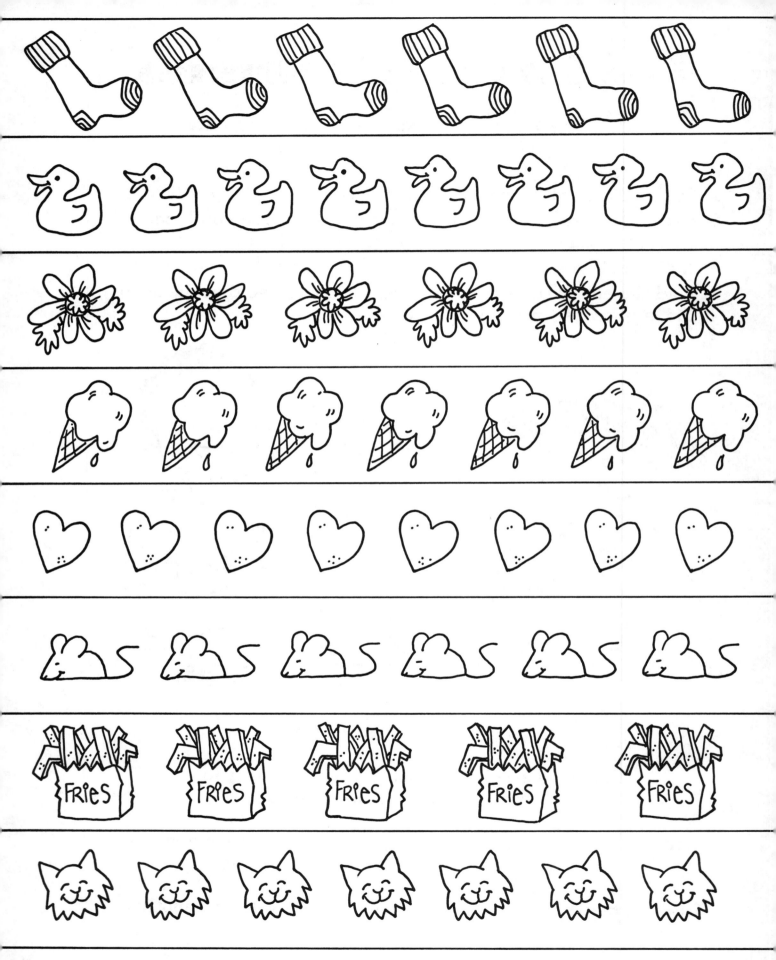

Nature's Paintbrush

Use the word bank below to complete the rhymes in the poem.

Word Bank

blue	light
bees	black
night	back
too	trees

Brilliant colors, red and pink,

Green and orange and _____.

Lovely shades of violet,

Brown and yellow _____.

Was it hard to find a brush

Small enough to paint the _____

Of a ladybug with tiny, tiny

Little dots of _____?

I love the silver glitter

That shines the stars at _____,

And the gold of yellow daffodils

You sprinkle with sun_____.

I giggle at your funny stripes

On zebras, snakes, and _____.

But I think you use your paint box best

To paint the autumn _____.

My Name Is _____

Say It with Pictures

Read this picture story aloud to yourself.

Now use the picture squares to create a funny rebus story
of your own.
Color the pictures you plan to use.
Then cut on the dotted lines to remove them from the page.
Arrange them on your paper in the order they need to be placed
to tell your story.
Use the empty squares to add extra words or pictures needed
to complete your story.

Messages for Mom and Dad

Follow the directions to create a unique card for Dad or Mom.
Decorate the shirt or blouse with real fabric, beads, and buttons.
Use crayons, markers, or scraps of fabric or paper
to make a tie or bow.
Write a love letter on the inside of the card.

Shirt

1. Cut on the solid line.
2. Fold on the dotted line.
3. Turn the page so that the fold is at the top.
4. Cut a two-inch-long horizontal slit, starting about three inches in from each side edge.
5. Cut about one inch down the center of one side of the shirt, starting from the slit you just made.
6. Bend the flaps to make a collar, as shown in the drawing.

Blouse

1. Follow Shirt Directions 1, 2, and 3.
2. Cut a crescent shape from the fold as shown.
3. Decorate with beads or a bow.

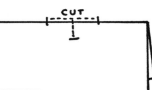

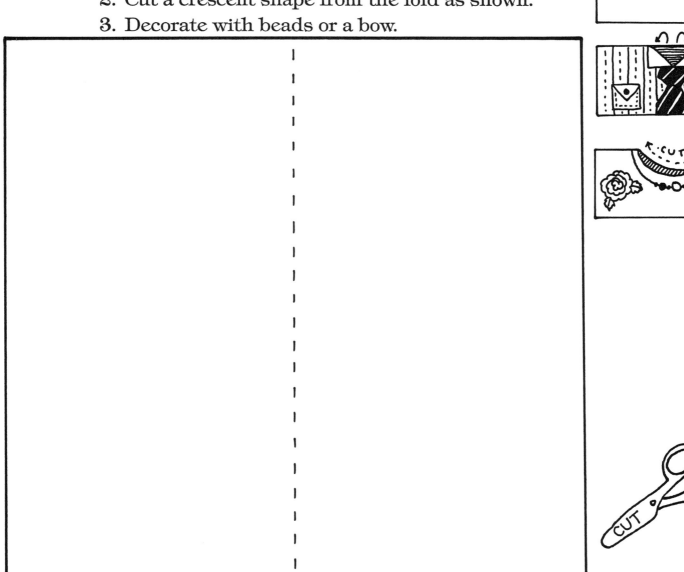

Stretch and Bend

Ask someone to take a stretch break with you.
First, you give the directions below
as both you and your friend follow the directions.

Stand up straight.
Let your arms hang down straight beside your body.
Stretch as "tall" as you can.
Raise your hands high over your head.
Clap your hands twice.
Now clap your hands three times.
Bend to the floor.
Touch the floor with your hands.
Stand up straight.
Turn your body around three times.
Hold your hands in front of your body.
Clap your hands three times.
Let your arms fall flat to your side.

Then, ask your friend to make up a set of directions
for both of you to follow.

44

Stretch to the Pictures

Now ask your friend to help you read the picture directions to
stretch and bend some other parts of your body.

Lace and Tie

Color the shoe.
Paste this page on a piece of tagboard or heavy construction paper.
Carefully cut out the shoe.
Use a paper punch to make a hole on each X.
Use yarn or a shoelace to lace and tie a perfect bow on your shoe!

Category Catch-up

See how many of these directions you can complete
in fifteen minutes.

- Make an X on each of the pictures that is smaller than
  the cookie.
- Draw a circle around every picture that is larger than
  the doll.
- Make a square box around every picture whose name
  begins with the letter C.
- Draw a dotted line to connect three pictures whose
  names rhyme with bat.
- Color the pictures of seven living things.

My Name Is _____

Crow Calls a Meeting

Color the animal pictures.
Follow the dotted lines to cut out the animal shapes.
Paste each animal in its proper place on the picture page.
Color the remainder of the picture.
Tell about the conversation you might hear if the animals
could talk among themselves.

48

My Name Is _____

49

A Nose for Prose

Follow the directions to make bookmarks that will keep your nose in a book at just the right place!

1. Color the bookmarks.

2. Paste the whole bookmark part of this page on a piece of tagboard or lightweight cardboard.

3. Cut out the bookmarks. Then follow the dotted lines to cut carefully around the nose on each bookmark.

4. Decorate with scraps of colored paper, yarn, and ribbon.

5. Place each bookmark in one of your favorite books. Hang the nose over the page on which you will begin reading.

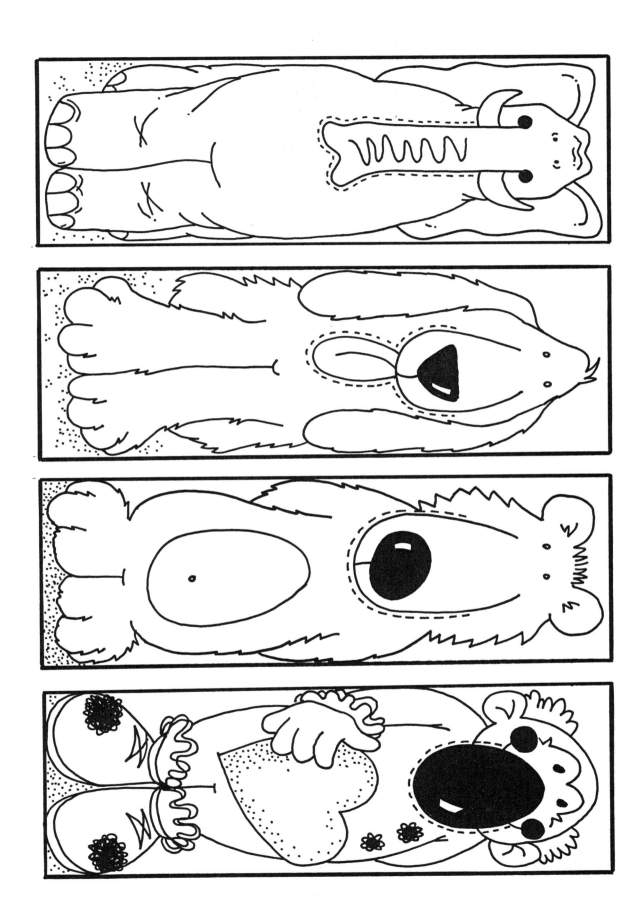

Name Crazy

It's fun to see your name written in an unusual way.
Follow the directions to create your name in crazy patterns and
colors or, if you wish, in three dimensions!

1. Looking at the ABC letters, locate each letter of your first name.
2. Cut out those letters and copy or enlarge them if you wish.
3. Color them "crazy."
4. Mount them on a piece of wood or cardboard in a crazy line to make a cockeyed name plate, like this:

For a 3-D Name:

1. Cut two of each letter shape.
2. Use a needle and yarn or a stapler to fasten the two shapes together, but leave a "stuffing hole" where you stuff cotton balls or tissue paper to make your letter fat and puffy.

3. Then attach the letters to one another in order by stapling one small portion of each letter to the letter that belongs on either side of it. Make it look crazy like this:

52

Kool Shades

Sometimes things just get too hard or too wild,
and you need a rest.
When that happens, you can put on these "kool shades"
to block out the rest of the world and enjoy
a few minutes of calm and quiet.
You might also use the shades during your rest time at school.

1. Use the pattern to cut your "kool shade" mask from a fabric such as soft cotton, felt, or fake fur.
2. Decorate your mask with fabric scraps, ribbons, buttons, sequins, or fake eyelashes.
3. Punch a hole in each side of the mask and attach yarn ties or an elastic band to keep your mask in place.
4. Put on your "kool shades" and take five!

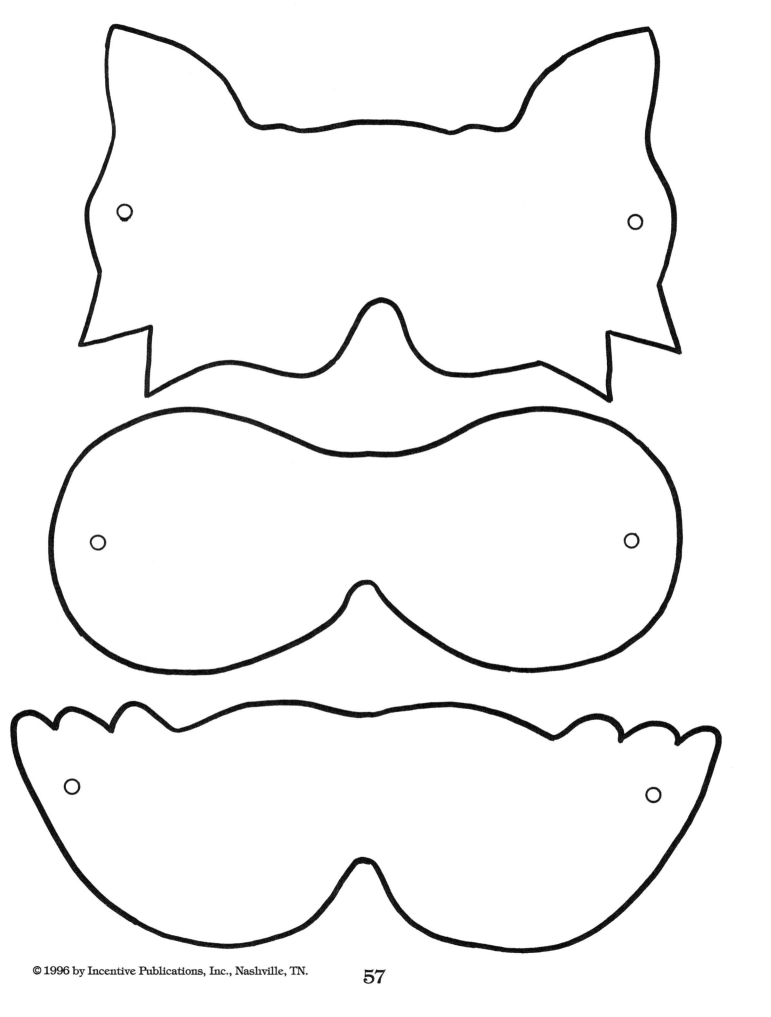

Circus Train

Follow the directions to make your own circus train.

1. For each animal you wish to include in your circus train, use a piece of 8"x 10" posterboard.
2. Put bars on the posterboard by using strips of masking tape.
3. Use a pencil to draw one of your favorite circus animals on each piece of posterboard. (Draw right over the tape as if it were not there.)
4. Color or paint your circus animal.
5. When the picture is dry, carefully pull off the masking tape.
6. Make as many copies as needed of the cage frame on the next page.
7. Color the frames.
8. Cut out the blank space in the center of each frame.
9. Paste one frame over each animal cage.
10. Display your circus train on a wall or bulletin board.

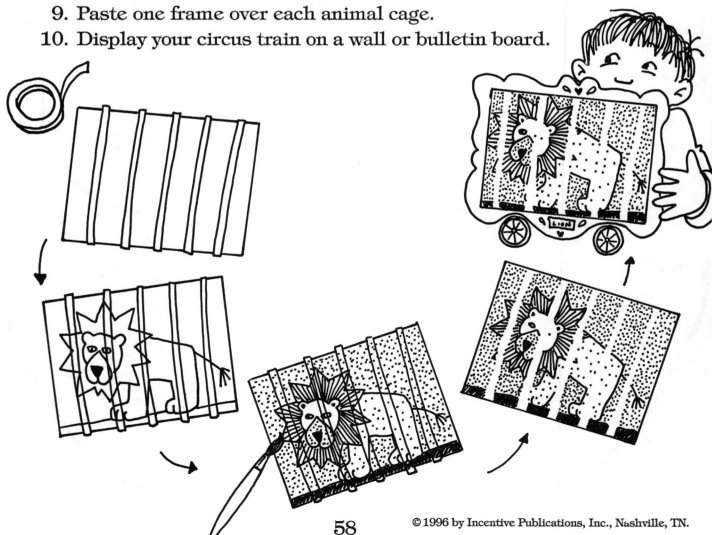

Baby Bear's Summer Dream

To write about Baby Bear's dream, put the circled letters
in numerical order on the lines below.

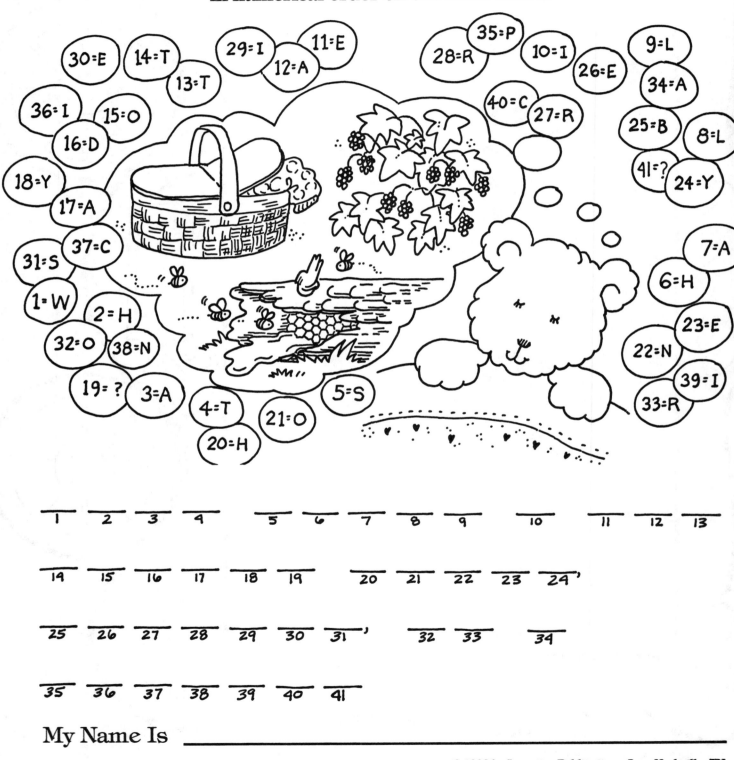

My Name Is _____

Curly, Come-alive Fish

Tell a friend you can make a fish come alive in her hands!
Your friend probably won't believe you, so try this!

1. Use the fish pattern on this page to cut a fish shape from a piece of plastic. (The kind of plastic container used for take-out food at the grocery store is perfect!)
2. Be sure your fish has a large fancy tail!
3. Tell your friend to rub his or her hands together so that they are very warm. Then ask your friend to hold out that hand and place the fish in the center of the palm.
4. Watch the fish. Within a few seconds, the fish will begin to curl its tail toward its head !

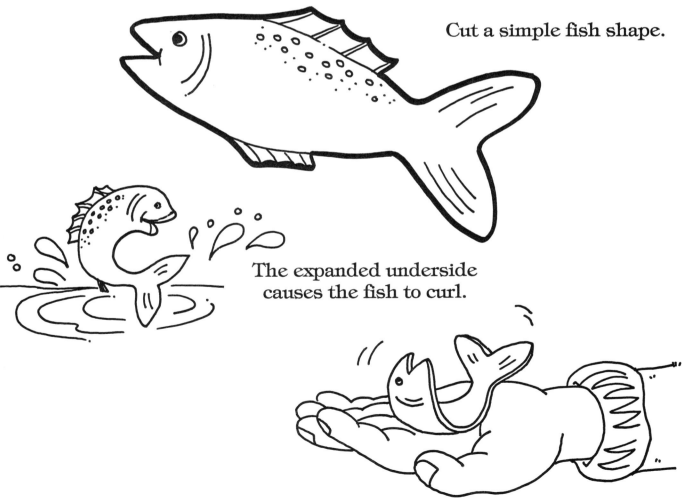

Cut a simple fish shape.

The expanded underside causes the fish to curl.

Treasure Hunt

Use the clue tags below to set up a treasure hunt for
a friend or a group of classmates.
You may fill in each blank with either a word or a picture that
tells the hunter(s) where to look for the next clue.

1. Begin with clue #1. Think about where you want to send your hunter to look for clue #2. Write the name of that place or draw a picture of it.
2. Decide where the next clue tag will be hidden, and write the name or draw a picture of that place on clue #2.
3. Continue with as many clue tags as you wish until you are ready to send the hunter to the treasure.
4. The last clue will show the hunter where to look for the treasure.

The treasure may be a tasty treat that all the hunters can share.
Or it may be a toy or a trinket or something special that
you made yourself!

CLUE # 1

GO TO _____

CLUE # 2

GO TO _____

CLUE # 3

GO TO _____

CLUE # 4

GO TO _____

CLUE #5

    GO TO _____

CLUE # 6

    GO TO _____

CLUE # 7

    GO TO _____

CLUE # 8

    GO TO _____

CLUE # 9

    GO TO _____

CLUE #10

    GO TO _____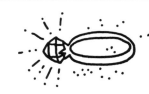

LOOK HERE FOR THE TREASURE!

Zoo-boree!

This game is for two players.
Ask a special person to play it with you.

1. Provide a die and buttons, pebbles, or bottle tops for markers.

2. To begin the game, each player should place a marker on the "Free Passes Today" space.

3. Allow the person you invited to play with you to play first. He or she throws the die and moves the correct number of spaces.

4. The player must read the message in the space and do what the message says before the other player can count to ten. The other player may start counting as soon as the marker is placed in the space.

5. If the player reads the message and follows the directions, he or she may move ahead one space (unless the marker landed on a space that says "go back" or "lose a turn"). If the player does not follow the directions, that player must go back two spaces.

6. The first player to reach the "exit" space wins the game.

64

ZOO-BOREE!

Free Passes Today!

ADMIT ONE ZOO ADMIT ONE

You are BARELY on your way MOVE AHEAD 1 SPACE

Tell how many are in the cage.

Name 3 animals whose names begin with the letter G.

Go Back one space.

Describe this interesting bird.

Count the humps. Move that many spaces ahead.

ZOO DETOUR! Jump back to the mother.

You are almost there. Rest here until next turn.

EXIT

Tell one thing special about this animals babies.

BE CREATIVE. Name 2 words that rhyme with ZOO.

Name one snack you might buy.

SNACKS

POP CANDY

Tell a Picture Story

First, the mother bird builds a nest.
This mother bird has a nest all ready.

In box #1, draw two eggs.

In box #2, draw two birds.

In box #3, draw a worm for the baby birds.

In box #4, draw one bird flying away.

In box #5, draw the other bird flying away.

Look at box #6 and tell the story your pictures show.

My Name Is _____

Easy-to-fix Fruitpicks

Read the directions and gather your supplies to make
a healthy treat. These directions will make eight Fruitpicks.

You will need:

8 toothpicks
8 miniature marshmallows
8 pineapple chunks
8 maraschino cherries

Directions:

1. Stick one pineapple chunk on each toothpick.

2. Next to the pineapple chunk, stick one miniature marshmallow.

3. Push one maraschino cherry next to the miniature marshmallow.

Place your Fruitpicks on a pretty paper plate and share them with friends.

A Funny, Funny Garden

Follow the directions to find some funny things hiding in this picture.

1. Look in the tree for an animal that should be somewhere else.
2. Color the animal brown.
3. Draw a line from the animal to its home.
4. Search the flowers for an animal pretending to be a flower.
5. Draw a box around the pretender.
6. Look carefully at a funny, funny flower.
7. Color the flower.
8. Find and circle two other funny, funny things hiding in the grass.

Tell a story about this funny, funny garden.

My Name Is _____

Who Goes There?

Use the patterns to make foot shapes that will create
mysterious paths to follow.

1. Find a piece of lightweight cardboard (the kind that is
   attached to the back of a tablet).
2. On the cardboard, trace three or four of the same footprints
   and cut them out.
3. Paste the footprints on a strip of paper and let the glue dry.
4. Fasten the strip around an old rolling pin or a glass bottle.
5. Roll the pin or bottle in a shallow pan of water-based paint.
6. Then roll it across a piece of paper. Voilà! You have a path of
   footprints.
7. Use your roller to make a long path of mysterious footprints to
   follow to a treasure.

Write a mystery story about where the footprints might take you
if you followed them.

70   © 1996 by Incentive Publications, Inc., Nashville, TN.

Philharmonic Fun

Invite a group of friends to join you in pretending to be an orchestra.

1. Divide yourselves into four sections: violins, clarinets, trumpets, and drums.
2. Let the people in each section experiment to discover an appropriate sound for the section (humming, buzzing, tooting, etc.). Practice the sounds and mime the motions used to play each group of instruments.

3. Choose a favorite recorded song. Play the tape and let each group of instruments practice playing along.

4. Choose a conductor. When the conductor pantomimes the playing of a particular instrument, that section of the orchestra plays along with the music. When the conductor waves his or her hands, all sections play together.

Players must watch the conductor carefully
in order to know when to play.

Percussion Only

Now pretend your orchestra has only percussion instruments.

1. All the percussion sounds are provided by the human body. Try these: stomp, clap, tap, slap, knock, snap, sniff, cluck.
2. Choose a conductor who models a rhythm pattern using combinations of several "body percussion instruments." A conductor might:
   - stomp her foot once
   - clap his hands twice
   - slap her thigh three times
   - knock on his head three times
   - snap her fingers once
3. The whole orchestra should then mimic the conductor.
4. Choose simple, easy patterns at first. Then graduate to more complicated ones.
5. Change conductors now and then.

A "Bee Proud" Mobile

Follow the directions to make a "Bee Proud" mobile.
You will need scissors, string, and a coat hanger.

- Cut out the bees.
- Cut pieces of string into different lengths.
- When you do something to "bee proud" of, write it on a bee.
- Punch a hole in the bee.
- Tie one end of a piece of string through the hole.
- Tie the other end of the string to the hanger.
- Continue this until all the bees are tied to the hanger.
- Hang your mobile and "bee proud."

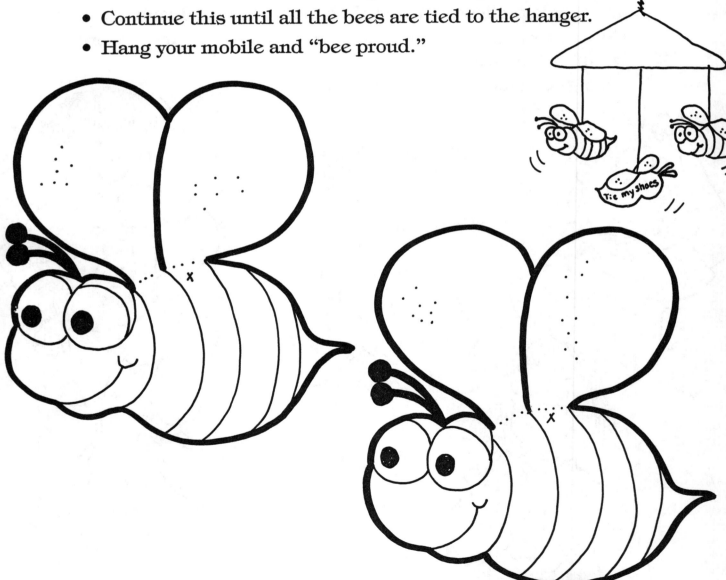

 # Teacher Notes

Take a Break

Keep a special box or jar in which you will place slips of paper, each suggesting three or four simple directions to be followed in sequence. Explain to students that these are brief, take-a-break activities for them to do between their academic work sessions. When a student finishes the workbook and reading assignment, he or she may leave the desk, draw a slip from the jar, and follow the directions. This activity not only provides practice in reading and following directions, but gives the student an opportunity to relax between intensive tasks.

Example:
1. Stretch your hands high to the sky.
2. Smile at the ceiling.
3. Sit down and go limp.
4. Now, wake up and go to work.

Talking Turkey

About a week before the Thanksgiving holiday, place the body of a large, colorful cardboard turkey on a wall or bulletin board. Give at least one large cardboard tail feather to each student and ask the student to write on the tail feather his or her own formula or set of directions for doing well in school. (An aide may have to assist nonreaders and non-writers.)

Holiday Planning

Work together as a class to prepare a menu of foods that students would like to eat at a holiday feast. Ask each student to choose one item from the menu and to write his or her own recipe for that item. (The recipes cannot be guaranteed to work, but they should be great fun to read and share!)

Smock Tops

Before beginning a messy project, provide a large supply of paper grocery bags, heavy yarn, scissors, tape, and crayons. Ask students to use these materials to design and create smock tops to wear for protecting their clothing during the project. Each will do this project a little differently. When they are finished, ask each student to model his or her creation and to give the class step-by-step instructions for making a smock top just like it.

Twin Pictures

Give each student a copy of two very simple pictures that are exactly the same. Ask the student to color the pictures so that no part of one picture is the same color as the same part of the other picture. Ask students to exchange twin pictures and check each other's work to be sure each has accurately followed the directions.

Listen to the Leader

Give all students a copy of the same simple picture. Select one student to stand before the class and give one simple instruction to alter or color the picture. All other students listen and follow the direction. Then appoint another student to issue a second directive to be followed by all students. Continue this process as long as time permits and as long as constructive directions are being given and followed. Then arrange students in a circle so they can all hold up their finished products and compare them for accuracy.

Popcorn Performance

When there is a slow or restless moment in the classroom, provide relief and help everyone to refocus by playing this game. Give very short directives, one at a time, in as rapid succession as possible. See how quickly everyone can comply.

Example: Snap your fingers. Touch your toes. Make your lips form an O shape. Use your body to make a T shape. Blink your eyes five times. Stick out your tongue. Wiggle like a worm. Make your hair stand straight on end. Put your finger in your left ear. Make a growling sound.

High-low, Top to Toe

Ask children to stand. Tell them that when they hear you sing or play a high note, they are to reach up to the tippy tops of their heads; when you sing or play a low note, they are to touch their toes. Repeat as time allows. Children can take turns being the leader, too.

Find the Treat

Hide a simple object such as a small toy, balloon, lollipop, or other treat in an easily accessible location. Write a set of directions for the child to follow to locate the surprise. Read the directions to the child and allow time for unhurried exploration and decision making.

Monthly Calendar

Use the monthly activity calendar on page 78 to reinforce the child's growth in learning to follow directions. Post the calendar in an easily accessible spot. Assist the child in interpreting and following the instructions for the day. Mark off each activity as completed with a star or other appropriate mark. At the end of the month, one of the awards on page 79 may be presented in recognition of the child's efforts.

76

Listen and Do

Giving a series of verbal directions for the child to follow helps the child develop good listening skills as well as provides practice in following directions.

Make worksheets with simple matching, labeling, categorizing, counting, coloring, pasting, or read-and-draw activities. Give the child verbal directions for completing the activities. Example:

Color the pictures of three jungle animals. Mark an X on the other animal.

elephant   whale   tiger   giraffe

Draw a circle around three farm animals. Color the other animal brown.

cow   pig   kangaroo   goat

Color the animals whose names rhyme. Name an animal that you would like
for a pet.

snake   cat   bat   rat

Provide plenty of time for discussion of each completed worksheet.

As the child achieves success with following simple directions, more complex directions involving an increased number of steps may be given.

Draw a circle, a square, an oval, a rectangle, and a triangle on the board. Discuss each shape with the children to make sure they can distinguish between the shapes. Then give instructions such as the following:

1. Draw three triangles at the top of your paper.
2. Draw six circles below the triangles.
3. Draw a big square, a middle-sized square, and a small square.
4. Draw four ovals.
5. Draw three rectangles at the bottom of your paper.

After the drawings are completed, give directions such as the following:

1. Color two triangles green.
2. Color one triangle red.
3. Make a box around all but two of the circles.
4. Draw lines to connect all of the squares.
5. Draw "faces" in the ovals.

To give more relevance to the activity, the shapes to draw may be planned to form an image that is seasonal or related to a current holiday or classroom topic.

After successful completion of an activity of this nature, the "Good Listener" badge on page 79 might be awarded.

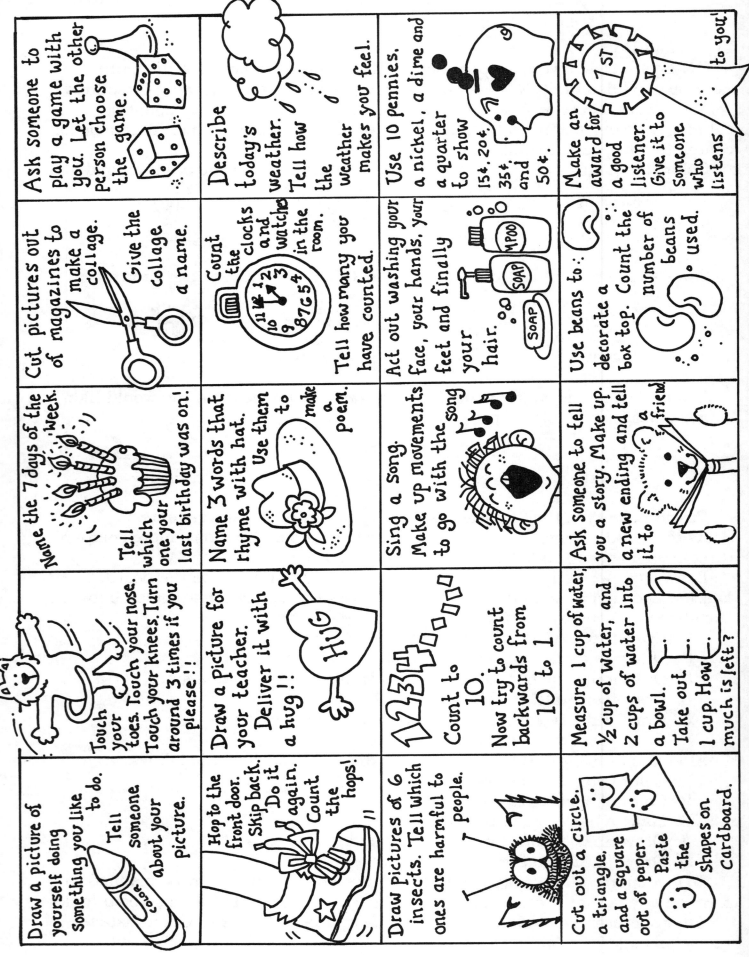

Ask someone to play a game with you. Let the other person choose the game.

Describe today's weather. Tell how the weather makes you feel.

Use 10 pennies, a nickel, a dime and a quarter to show 15¢, 20¢, 35¢, and 50¢.

Make an award for a good listener. Give it to someone who listens to you!

Cut pictures out of magazines to make a collage. Give the collage a name.

Count the clocks and watches in the room. Tell how many you have counted.

Act out washing your face, your hands, your feet and finally your hair.

Use beans to decorate a box top. Count the number of beans used.

Name the 7 days of the week. Tell which one your last birthday was on!

Name 3 words that rhyme with hat. Use them to make a poem.

Sing a Song. Make up movements to go with the song.

Ask someone to tell you a story. Make up a new ending and tell it to a friend.

Touch your toes. Touch your nose. Touch your knees. Turn around 3 times if you please!!

Draw a picture for your teacher. Deliver it with a hug!! HUG

Count to 10. Now try to count backwards from 10 to 1.

Measure 1 cup of water. ½ cup of water, and 2 cups of water into a bowl. Take out 1 cup. How much is left?

Draw a picture of yourself doing something you like to do. Tell someone about your picture.

Hop to the front door. Skip back. Do it again. Count the hops!

Draw pictures of 6 insects. Tell which ones are harmful to people.

Cut out a circle, a triangle, and a square out of paper. Paste the shapes on cardboard.

78   ©1996 by Incentive Publications, Inc., Nashville, TN.

GOOD LISTENER AWARD!

SUPER

CAN LISTEN AND FOLLOW DIRECTIONS

is a

SUPER
DIRECTION·FOLLOWER

remembered to
★ STOP
★ LOOK
★ LISTEN
★ THINK
and followed directions today!!